Peace in the Storm

Peace in the Storm

*Looking to God
When Your Child
is an Addict*

Kathie Flanders

XULON PRESS

Xulon Press
2301 Lucien Way #415
Maitland, FL 32751
407.339.4217
www.xulonpress.com

© 2020 by Kathie Flanders

All rights reserved solely by the author. The author guarantees all contents are original and do not infringe upon the legal rights of any other person or work. No part of this book may be reproduced in any form without the permission of the author. The views expressed in this book are not necessarily those of the publisher.

Unless otherwise indicated, Scripture quotations taken from the Holy Bible, New International Version (NIV). Copyright © 1973, 1978, 1984, 2011 by Biblica, Inc.™. Used by permission. All rights reserved.

Printed in the United States of America.

ISBN-13: 978-1-63221-748-6

Table of Contents

Light 1

Christ, My Shepherd. 5

The Mother Eagle 9

The Storm 13

Truth 17

Perseverance 21

Just Because I Can't See It. 25

Resentments 29

Heartbreak. 33

Holidays 37

Our Lost Sheep. 41

Speaking the Truth in Love. 45

Spiritual Malady 49

Emotional Pain 53

God's Forgiveness 57

Detachment. 61

Waiting 65

Disciplined 69

Wisdom. 73

From Fear to Peace 77

Healing and Hope. 81

Acknowledgments

My heartfelt thanks to:

God for His direction and patience with me in this writing process.

My husband Dick, who has always been my supporter and encourager in any challenge I take on.

Those who gave me editing feedback, prayer, and encouragement.

Those with a similar journey with an addicted child and for our times of shared hope in the Lord.

All my sisters in the Lord and my church family for your example of living for Christ that continues to inspire me.

Pastor Dennis Simmons, a faithful mentor and fellow believer in the power of Jesus Christ.

My friends and family, who have supported me in so many ways through the years.

Introduction
Peace in the Storm

God has helped me find peace in the storm.

A storm may be coping with cancer, a loved one's death, dealing with chronic pain, or living in a challenging relationship.

One of the most substantial storms for me to deal with in my life has been my journey having an adult child with addiction issues.

We have heard it said, "God does not give us more than we can handle." We may question that. Actually, God does give us more than we can handle, more than we can handle by ourselves—that is the point. If we could handle it, why would we need God? Why would we turn to God? God is wanting us to turn to Him. In our humanness and self-assuredness, we can have the attitude that we are all set without God. We can get ourselves through life. I believe we are created to seek to have a relationship with a higher power. God is never giving up on having that intimate relationship He created us to have with Him, acknowledging Him as the One who helps us through our storms, not ourselves.

I have moved from being in turmoil because someone dear's life was out of control to having peace with Christ, even though her life continues to be in chaos.

We can move from being in turmoil to having peace with Christ.

God is helping me learn how to accept my daughter's life as an addict—unsettled, chaotic, unhealthy—and to have that co-exist with my peaceful life in Christ. To me, that has been a series of miracles that at one time, I would not have thought possible.

Light

"…God is light, and in Him is no darkness at all."
(1 John 1:5b)

"Thy Word is a lamp unto my feet, and a light unto my path."(Psalm 119:105)

Light is an interesting thing. We can easily take it for granted, until we don't have it. It's funny how just a little light can help so much. One time when I couldn't sleep, I was finding my way around in our kitchen in the middle of the night. The only light was the tiny light that came from the stove clock, enabling me to see but just in shadows. I was aided in finding my way around because I already knew where things were in the kitchen. What a difference light can make! If even a little light is helpful, although things might be distorted, how much more would full light help?

The Word of God is like light. We can find our way through our problems, decision-making, and what steps to take next when we have light. Also, it dawned on me as I was making my way around the kitchen in the dark by memory that we make decisions by what we have done in the past, instead of with new light.

How often we try to make our way from a very small light. We see the way in shadows and try to make out the rest. God wants to lead our lives with light. He wants to flood our lives with new light. He has plenty of light to shine on our path to show us the way. How do we receive that light?—by reading Scripture and Christian literature and listening to Christian leaders. Light helps us with fear; it gives perspective, and we learn that light comes from a source greater than ourselves. How different things look in the light!

Prayer

Dear Lord, help us to avail ourselves of light that You have for us in Your Word by Your grace and love. As we deal with challenges and circumstances beyond our control, assist us in learning how to lean on You for direction.

Light

Is there something you feel in the dark about? In what way might you get more light in your life?

Christ, My Shepherd

"For the Son of man came to seek and to save the lost." (Luke 19:10)

"When He saw the crowds, He had compassion on them, because they were harassed and helpless, like sheep without a shepherd." (Matthew 9:36)

THESE VERSES PROVIDE QUITE A VISUAL FOR me. I picture an under-nourished lamb lost in the woods. His group has left the area. He's on his own. He has many things going against him. Nightfall isn't far away. He can hear the wolves. He is still hungry and so tired. I have felt like that lamb!

Lost can take on a variety of forms. We can feel lost when there is transition in our lives. We can feel lost when we have disappointments and when we suffer tragedies. People can be lost when they feel alone. God does not want us to be lost. He knows we need a shepherd to lead us.

When we are at our point of need and we cry out to God, He is always there for us. As we stay close to God, we get our needs met, and our faith in God and our love for Him grows. To see ourselves go from being that lost lamb with so many needs to a spiritually, physically, and emotionally healthy person is nothing short of a miracle!

Prayer

Dear Lord, help us to accept You, that You will be the shepherd of our lives. Help us to follow You and listen to Your compassionate heart for us.

Will you let God be your shepherd?

The Mother Eagle

"Trust in the Lord with all your heart and lean not on your own understanding. In all your ways acknowledge Him and He will direct your path." (Proverbs 3:5-6)

When an eagle is a baby, it is not able to care for itself. The mother eagle prepares a beautiful nest for her young where it is safe and secure. As it grows older, it outgrows the nest; the mother must prepare for the young to leave the nest and learn to fly. When the air current is just right for the wings to catch, the young eagle ventures out of the nest and gets caught in the wind current and *wow*, it is flying! Not far away, the mother eagle is watching.

Just like the mother eagle, our Heavenly Father is not far away. He is aware of all things, including changes in the wind patterns and possible dangers to us. We can trust Him. He will direct us.

Peace in the Storm

When new things come into our lives, it's like needing to leave our nest; we need to leave our comfort zone. If the eagle never left its comfort zone, it would never learn to fly. What kind of life would an eagle have without being able to fly? God the Creator planned for the eagle to fly.

Just like with us, we must leave our comfort zone to reach our potential and trust God for what He has prepared for us. With the mother eagle, she knows her young cannot stay in the nest for the rest of their lives. They must learn to fly; they will outgrow the nest. If her young do not leave the nest on their own, she makes the nest uncomfortable. She may flap her wings on them to get them to leave the nest; she forces them to test their wings. The young eagles may not want to leave the nest, so she essentially pushes them out for their own good. As they leave the nest to learn to fly, the mother flies below them so that if they were to fall, she would catch them.

So it is with the Lord as we understand from His Word. He may at times do the same with us. It may seem as if He has given us more than we can handle—we are being pushed outside our comfort zone for a reason. He has not deserted us!

The Mother Eagle

We can be like the baby eagles who do not want to leave the comfort and security of what we know so well. We are cozy and settled. However, our Creator knows what is best for us, and as we outgrow where we are at, we need to leave our comfort zone, just like the young eagles need to leave their nest to learn to fly. What kind of an eagle would it be if it couldn't soar and do what God created it to do?

Prayer

Dear Lord, guide us in how to be willing to leave our comfort zones. Help us to trust You with the unknowns in our lives and to have faith that You are caring for us.

How are we like the eagle who doesn't want to leave the comfort and security of the nest? What might we be missing that God has in store for us?

A Storm

"The Lord is my strength and my shield, my heart trusted in Him and I am helped, therefore my heart greatly rejoices and with my song I will praise Him." (Psalm 28:7)

"In the world you will have tribulation, but be of good cheer, I have overcome the world." (John 16:33)

I REMEMBER ONE OF THE FIRST TIMES I accepted God's peace in the middle of the storm. It was new; it was different because the matter wasn't settled yet. I had not heard that my child was okay. I had been unable to sleep. The last conversation with my daughter had not gone well, but God gave me His peace and hope.

I don't particularly like reading Scripture or embracing the idea that I will have hardship. Like many others, I prefer things to be pleasant, pleasurable, fun, etc. Perhaps in some situations, it's not human nature to submit ourselves readily to growth opportunities or environments that come from affliction.

However, much of Scripture presents the idea that we will have tribulation as Christ's followers—we can expect it. The good news for us that takes faith is trusting that Christ is in control.

I find it interesting that obedience to Him, what I am supposed to be doing, ends up being the answer or my way through the hardship. God's plan is to keep us and give us His peace in the storm, not remove the storm or remove us from the storm. What I can do in a storm is trust God and His promises. Resting in God's peace makes a statement that I trust God and His timing, that I am confident that God has things under control.

So not only with Christ do we make it through our trial but we are victorious in that we learn to allow God's peace to direct us. As I spend time in the Word, I reflect on God's character, His promises, and His plan.

Prayer

Dear Lord, help us to see how we can grow through our struggles. Help us to be obedient and to allow You to work in us.

A Storm

How do we live with peace in Christ on the one hand and crisis on the other hand?

Truth

"If you hold to my teaching, you are really my disciples. Then you will know the truth and the truth will set you free." (John 8:31-32)

"If the Son sets you free, you will be free indeed." (John 8:36)

I AM FRUSTRATED, ANGRY, UPSET, DISAP-pointed, and resentful! I expected she would have taken advantage of one of the opportunities presented to her to get help and change her life for the better.

I want her to have a life in Christ, a person experiencing His peace. I want her to have quality time and a healthy relationship with her children. I want her to have a church family. I want so much for her.

What I see is that I get overwhelmed with my feelings. I become all about what I want for her, what I expect her to do. Of course, this sounds like what you would expect of a parent; but what God has shown me is that it is a lot about me. I am uncomfortable with her lifestyle. There is no freedom for me in this. It's about me learning to trust God when things are not moving at the speed I want them to. With my relationship with Christ, I find that there is a peace that comes with admission of reality, with being truthful about feelings and truthful before God.

Christ helps us in that although the truth is not what we want, it is reality, and it has to be dealt with. It means letting go of my timetable and trusting God's plan and timetable.

God always has things for us to learn. He is teaching me to have faith and to not stop praying for my daughter. She needs to take steps that she just isn't ready to take to obtain these things. With God's help, I know it is possible.

My prayer is for my daughter to experience the freedom this scripture talks about: "If the Son sets you free, you will be free indeed" (John 8:36)—this grace that God gives when we turn our lives over to Him completely.

Prayer

Dear Lord, teach me how to be honest with You and to accept the truth from You. I pray for my addicted loved one that he/she will find the truth of freedom in Christ.

Truth

What are signs I can pick up on that I am not dealing honestly with reality? How can I do a better job of that starting today?

Perseverance

"Consider it pure joy, my brothers and sisters, whenever you face trials of many kinds, because you know that the testing of your faith produces perseverance. Let perseverance finish its work so that you may be mature and complete not lacking anything."
(James 1:2-4)

Who is mature and complete, not lacking anything? Certainly not I! I struggle with it being pure joy when I face a trial. However, I have heard what James is suggesting is that "we consider". Perhaps that means work toward it—make it a goal.

Perseverance will need to continue to finish its work until God takes me home. It would appear facing trials and the testing of our faith will continue to occur. Do we wait to experience joy when we are mature and complete, when we have no trials? Evidently not, as verse 2 states, "Consider it pure joy when you face trials"! Perhaps consider could mean that although it may not be our first reaction as humans, James encourages us as Christ's followers to work toward, think about, or contemplate that these trials are a thing to be joyful about because of the results they bring. We know the outcome will be spiritual growth. God is working in us.

As humans, we will face trials and will need to figure out a way to get through them. "The Lord will keep you from all harm, he will watch over your life, the Lord will watch over your coming and going both now and forevermore" (Ps. 121:7). So, we would say to James, what about our trial, our pain and hardship? Well, we come to believe and understand that for these two concepts to co-exist, which they do, God does not mean trial to harm us; He means it for growth. God is not passively looking by! He is in control.

PRAYER

Dear Lord, help me to see that trials and heartache are meant to bring me close to You and to allow me to grow in my faith in You. Guide me in how to let You do Your work in my life. I submit to You and Your process for me.

Perseverance

What am I finding hard to deal with today? How can I see God working in and through that?

Just Because I Don't See the Answer

"Come to me, all you are weary and burdened, and I will give you rest. Take my yoke upon you and learn from me, for I am gentle and humble in heart, and you will find rest for your souls. For my yoke is easy and my burden is light." (Matthew 11:28-30)

I COULD HEAR THE NOISE, BUT I COULDN'T see the source. There wasn't any wind, and it didn't look like it was raining. Yet, as I opened the door to look outside, I could see that it was raining. It was a gentle yet steady rain that was making noise. I was reminded how God is working even when we don't think He is. His promises and His character tell us that.

It can be exhausting when nothing seems to change; when I don't see changes in my child's life, when I don't see answers to prayers, I can tend to think God isn't listening or God isn't working. I become worn out.

However, just because I don't see the answer doesn't mean God is not at work.

God beckons us to come to Him for rest. I can imagine a wooden yoke that supports and holds two oxen together—that our great God would be willing to wear a yoke with us, to help us, to teach us. It is a visual of not being alone and of having a way to make it through our troubles.

Prayer

Dear Lord, help me to come to You for rest and to be willing to learn from You.

Just Because I Don't See the Answer

Can I accept that God is working, even when I don't see it?

Resentments

"My dear brothers and sisters, take note of this: everyone should be quick to listen, slow to speak and slow to become angry." (James 1:19)

"Pursue peace with all people, and holiness, without which no one will see the Lord; looking carefully lest anyone fall short of the grace of God; lest any root of bitterness springing up cause trouble, and by this many become defiled." (Hebrews 12:14-15)

One way I can tell resentments are building is when I have the attitude, "Are you kidding me?" Resentments can come from expectations. When I am saying, "Are you kidding me?" I am saying I had other expectations in mind. I expect or think someone should say or do something differently than he or she did. It isn't unusual to have unrealistic expectations or resentments when you are the parent of an addict.

God does not want me to have resentments that can lead to anger or to an argument. In James, we learn we need to ask God to help us be quick to listen and slow to be angry. I have come to learn that dealing with resentments is my responsibility.

Anyone can be subject to having resentments. Resentments are a funny thing because we don't really want to admit they are our responsibility to avoid or to take care of. I haven't always wanted to admit I have them! They can be subtle. The real problem with resentments is that they don't just stay that way; they become something else. They morph and/or manifest themselves as self-pity or martyrdom or justified anger. Being aware that we have them can help. Adjusting our expectations can be a start.

Prayer

Dear Lord, please show me expectations and resentments I have. Teach me to be slow to anger and quick to listen.

Resentments

What do I tend to become resentful about? How can I allow God to help me with that?

Heartbreak

The Lord is close to the brokenhearted and saves those who are crushed in spirit."
(Psalm 34:18)

I AM HEARTBROKEN BECAUSE MY DAUGHTER is not in a good place. Her life is like a rollercoaster of chaos because of her addiction. She cannot see her way through it to the other side to have a life of peace. She must be heartbroken too! It's hard to concentrate on life, on functioning and keeping life in order when you are overwhelmed and your heart is breaking. God tells us He is close to us in times like these.

Heartbreak has caused me to want to escape because I just don't want to deal with pain. It has caused me to be sad and discouraged; because of heartbreak, I can find it hard to love. I have received help from God for my heartache. He knows how I feel and what I am going through.

"Praise be to the God and Father of our Lord Jesus Christ, the Father of compassion and the God of all comfort, who comforts us in all our troubles, so that we can comfort those in any trouble, with the comfort we ourselves receive from God" (2 Cor. 1:3-4).

With God's help, I have gotten used to living with heartache and heartbreak; even when nothing seems to change, God wants to be close to us to comfort us and revive us.

We will not go through this life without heartache. Thankfully, with God we have someone who cares about what we are dealing with. We can pour our hearts out to God, and He will listen and comfort us.

Sometimes God helps us by directing us to people or reading material or a particular scripture that is just what we need in our situation. Through this, our faith grows.

Prayer

Dear Lord, thank you that You care about my broken heart. I give You my broken heart today.

Heartbreak

Do I try to ignore my broken heart? What is the best thing for me to do with my broken heart?

Holidays

"Wait on the Lord, be of good courage, and He shall strengthen your heart; Wait I say on the Lord." (Psalm 27:14)

"Trust in the Lord with all your heart, and lean not on your own understanding; in all your ways acknowledge Him and He will direct your paths." (Proverbs 3:5-6)

This is not my first Christmas dealing with an addict's way of thinking around the holidays. It is such a challenge for addicts/alcoholics because they have so many mixed urges and emotions. Their addicted brains are telling them it's a legitimate reason to use substances, and for an addict, that means abusing them. The addict is overwhelmed with guilt and expectations.

I have tried to help my daughter and tried to control her behavior. Usually, this is not successful. The illogical and impulsive behavior, the poor decision-making and lack of responsibility are all part of the behavior of an addict.

I am finally seeing my way through all of it with God's help. I have learned that the most I can do sometimes is to minimize the whirlwind or merry-go-round effect the addict has on myself and other family members.

I would be certain my daughter does not see the effect on others. She is zeroed in on her world and her concerns. I can't imagine fully what it is like to be an addict or alcoholic around the holidays, whether you are in recovery or not.

As hard as it is to wait on the Lord, it pays off. I remember a particular time when my daughter had called me; she was in a tight spot due to her decision-making. I wanted to call her back, to try and help her, to figure out the mess she was in. I prayed and waited on God. I did not have a peace about calling her. I didn't have the answer. I continued to pray. Time passed, God worked, and I was obedient.

Taking a situation and purposefully praying about it and asking fellow believers to pray with you about it is really beneficial. God does strengthen our hearts.

This has become one of my favorite verses: "The Lord is my strength and my shield; my heart trusts in Him and He helps me. My heart leaps for joy, and with my song I praise Him" (Ps. 28:7).

Holidays

Prayer

Dear Lord, teach me how to trust You and how to wait on You.

Why do I have such a hard time waiting on the Lord?
In what ways do I need to wait on the Lord?

Our Lost Sheep

"Then Jesus told them this parable: Suppose one of you has a hundred sheep and loses one of them. Doesn't he leave the ninety-nine in the open country and go after the lost sheep until he finds it? And when he finds it, he joyfully puts it on his shoulders and goes home. Then he calls his friends and neighbors together and says, rejoice with me, I have found my lost sheep. I tell you that in the same way there will be more rejoicing in heaven over one sinner who repents than over ninety-nine righteous persons who do not need to repent." (Luke 15:3-7)

"When He saw the crowds, He had compassion on them, because they were harassed and helpless, like sheep without a shepherd. Then He said to his disciples, the harvest is plentiful but the workers are few. Ask the Lord of the harvest, therefore

to send out workers into his harvest field."
(Matthew 9:36-38)

MANY PEOPLE TODAY ARE LIKE THAT PASsage we read about the sheep without a shepherd—a herd of sheep who have had a bad season, no leader, not sure where they could go for water or food; some have been through the pucker brush, and their coats are dirty. They look lost, and they look pretty rough. Their wool is matted; they look undernourished. This group of sheep needs help! They need a leader. Sometimes our addicted children can seem like that.

In Jesus's time, crowds of people pursued Him. The lost followed Him; they came to Him in droves. They were sick, blind, hurt, and bankrupt spiritually. God in His mercy saw a flock without a shepherd and had compassion on them. People are still coming to Jesus today and receiving help. God is still a God of compassion. Our loved ones need God to step into their lives and heal, help, and save them.

PRAYER

Dear Lord, we pray for our lost sheep. We know how much You love them and pursue them. We pray You will bring harvesters into their lives and help bring them to You.

How can we point our children to the shepherd?

Speaking the Truth in Love

"A new command I give you: Love one another. As I have loved you, so you must love one another." (John 13:34)

"Then we will no longer be infants, tossed back and forth by the waves and blown here and there by every wind of teaching and by the cunning and craftiness of people in their deceitful scheming. Instead, speaking the truth in love, we will grow to become in every respect the mature body of Him who is the head, that is Christ." (Ephesians 4:14-15)

I DID NOT ALWAYS SPEAK THE TRUTH IN love to my addict daughter. I loved and nurtured and cared but did not speak the truth or even acknowledge the truth at times. As I continued to love and nurture without the truth, resentment settled in. After investing so much and not getting the desired results, I began to feel taken advantage of; I became disillusioned.

God was drawing me to Himself. He began speaking the truth into my life. I began listening. Then I began to speak the truth.

So I went from love without truth to truth only to the balance of speaking the truth in love in a timely way. For me, this took wisdom that comes from God.

The story of the conversation that Jesus had with the rich young man comes to mind (Matt. 19:16-22). This man asked Jesus what he needed to do to be sure he had secured his eternal destiny. Jesus shared that he needed to obey the commandments, to which the young man indicated he had; then Jesus shared that he needed to sell everything.

In this example, Jesus shared the truth in love; He stated the facts. The young man could accept what Jesus said; change or not change, it was his choice. Jesus did not plead or run after him; He did not make it easy or change the truth to accommodate this young man. He simply stated the truth in love.

Why is speaking the truth in love so hard, especially to an addict or alcoholic? Perhaps it's because we don't know what the response may be, or maybe we do know and we don't want to deal with it. It could be lip service (initial compliance, later proving to just be words) or a silent response or anger.

God's way of loving is different than our way of loving. With God, it is about what is in the heart. In Luke 6:45, we read, "A good man brings good things out of the good stored up in his heart, and an evil man brings evil things of the evil stored in his heart. For the mouth speaks what the heart is full of." God can give us a pure heart to love from.

Prayer

Dear Lord, we need Your help to speak the truth in love and to be willing to hear the truth from You. Lord, we will not stop praying for our children and for others that they will come to true repentance for that is love.

In what ways am I not being truthful? How can I begin to tell the truth in love?

Spiritual Malady

"Blessed is the one whose transgressions are forgiven; whose sins are covered. Blessed is the one whose sin the Lord does not count against them, in whose spirit is no deceit…I acknowledged my sin to you and did not cover up my iniquity. I said, I will confess my transgressions to the Lord and you forgave the guilt of my sin." (Psalm 32:1-2, 5)

DENIAL? PERHAPS SOME, BUT RECEIVING the news I had cancer did not shake me up that much. Was it because it was low grade? A friend said, "Kathie, it's still cancer." Why was it I wasn't more shook up? I knew I had peace because God is in control but there was more, then it dawned on me. I've had cancer before. I have dealt with it before, a cancer of a different sort—a spiritual cancer or malady, a spiritual illness. I look back to a time in my life where God was not in the management role. I was. I was separated from God. If God is not calling the shots, who is? Not led by God, left to human devices—this was not a pretty sight in my life. Separation from God equals a spiritual malady.

What is the remedy, the treatment for this spiritual malady?

Cancer of sin—the cancer of sin is caused by separation from God. Sin creates a gap between us and God. Can that gap be crossed? Who can bridge the gap? A most holy God—Jesus Christ is that God and bridged that gap.

When Jesus walked on this earth, He not only showed us the way; He is the way.

Jesus Christ bridged that gap so we can have a link to God on most high. Separation from God occurs when there is sin in our lives. In Him is no darkness; God does not abide with sin. The cure is to not be separated from God—to accept His love and His forgiveness, to accept help from a supportive, all wise, and all-powerful God.

No one wants to hear the news or face the fact he or she has cancer in his or her body. What are the dangers of not recognizing or not treating cancer? It may spread, it may get worse, and it could take a life.

No one wants to hear the truth about sin. What are the dangers of not recognizing and treating cancer of the spiritual nature? The same thing—the spiritual malady gets worse, leads to separation from God, and can lead to death spiritually.

God is good; God offers life.

Prayer

Dear Lord, teach us how to stay within the reaches of Your love. Help us to accept Your forgiveness and love and not be separated from You.

In what ways am I separated from God today? What is God's plan for me?

Emotional Pain

"May our Lord Jesus Christ Himself and God our Father, who loved us and by His grace gave us eternal encouragement and good hope, encourage your hearts and strengthen you in every good deed and word." (2 Thessalonians 2:16-17)

Have you ever felt like you would like to endure physical pain rather than emotional pain? Emotional pain for me is the aftermath of disagreements and of discouragement. I could not always identify the emotions I was dealing with like guilt, loss, and denial.

I would become disheartened and tired after opportunities I felt my addict daughter missed or treatment programs uncompleted. My hopes would be built up because my daughter acted and talked like she was going in the right direction. I extended myself; I would get my hopes up, only to be let down. Her addiction took her on a path that she could not get off of without the help of God.

My exhaustion or pain exhibit themselves in having problems sleeping or being frustrated or irritated easily. Sometimes I overreact, or I can be withdrawn.

I came to see that I needed to keep my eyes on Jesus, not the unsolved, ongoing issue of my daughter's addiction. God has power, and He has a plan. God has compassion and can heal! I prayed that God would give me faith, and He did! Only with God's grace do I have tolerance and compassion. I will not stop believing that my addict daughter and others dealing with addiction issues will come to Christ and receive the help they need to be free from their obsession and their destructive way of life.

I began to learn that God can't use me in my child's life if I am blinded by inappropriate feelings of guilt or overwhelmed with frustration. I must allow God to first help me with my emotional pain and exhaustion. I am learning to defer to God. I have no power except through Christ's power in me.

I also understand that addicts who are not allowing Christ to free them from their addictive behavior are going to be experiencing emotional pain.

Prayer

Dear Lord, help me to keep my eyes on You. Thank you for encouraging me and showing me Your love.

In what ways might I need to get in touch with my feelings and turn them over to God?

God's Forgiveness

"Blessed is the one whose transgressions are forgiven; whose sins are covered. Blessed is the one whose sin the Lord does not count against them, in whose spirit is no deceit…I acknowledged my sin to you and did not cover up my iniquity. I said, I will confess my transgressions to the Lord and you forgave the guilt of my sin." (Psalm 32:1-2, 5)

"I will instruct you and teach you in the way you should go. I will guide you with my eye." (Psalm 32:8)

"Rejoice in the Lord and be glad, you who are right with God; sing, all you are upright in heart." (Psalm 32:11)

WHAT A RELIEF GOD'S FORGIVENESS IS! Nothing else compares to it. For me, it can involve tears, tears of joy and peace. It results in an increase of faith.

It automatically resets you on a new course. To quote my mom in reference to God, "When you admit you are wrong, you are right; and you are in a right relationship with God."

We all make mistakes. We can all feel isolated or separated from God at times. Without accepting Christ's forgiveness, we can get weighed down, discouraged, and lose our way.

This is not God's plan for us. Our sins are forgiven; that is why Christ died on the cross—to take our sins away. As we move toward God, we have a fantastic opportunity to praise God for His marvelous provision of grace and be reminded of how our management of our lives falls short and how our lives under Christ's management are abundant lives. We can be in that very desired position before God of being humble and needy and at a total loss without God and His grace.

Prayer

Dear God, help us to acknowledge the truth in Scripture. God is more than able to help us with feelings of guilt or any feelings we have. Help us to be honest before You and allow You to remove anything that is separating us from You.

God's Forgiveness

What is separating you from God, and what do we read in Scripture about this?

Detachment

"For God has not given us the spirit of fear, but of power, and of love, and of a sound mind." (2 Timothy 1:7)

Detachment, or non-attachment, may sound like a strange thing to talk or think about in reference to an alcoholic/addict; I found it necessary—necessary for sanity and spiritual maintenance. I think I became more serious about detaching from my alcoholic daughter in a healthy way about ten years ago.

I can remember what it was like, not being detached. For me, it looked like this …her chaos or problems became mine. She would call me up around 7:00 am, perhaps a Monday morning, and need diapers, cigarettes, milk, etc. Could I please go purchase them and stop on my way to work at her place and drop them off? I did this a few times. A pattern was emerging. Soon it became apparent that she had been high or drunk on the weekend, misspent time and money, and knew I would be near her home Monday morning for work.

Detachment in reference to addiction issues can be the opposite of enabling. Enabling, I learned, is doing something for others that they can do for themselves, and it allows them to think their current behavior is not problematic. I have heard it said that detachment is neither kind nor unkind. It doesn't imply judgement of the person or situation we are detaching from. In my case, I chose to detach myself from the adverse effects of her abusing substances. Detachment allowed me to let go of my obsession with her behavior and lead my own life guided by God. In my case, detachment did not mean I stopped loving my addict; it means I stopped letting her behavior dictate my life.

God gave me strength and wisdom. Spending time in prayer and Scripture reading daily or as much as possible opened my eyes. For a short time, I attended Al-Anon meetings that helped me with my thinking. Detaching from, not enabling or rescuing, our addicts or alcoholics is not an easy task. It is not a task without heartbreak; however, I found it to be a necessary task. It is not a task that happens immediately; it's a lifestyle change that we make. I found it isn't something I do once and I am all set. I still catch myself enabling at times. It takes God's wisdom for me not to enable and to detach with love.

Prayer

Dear Lord, please help me to take the necessary steps to detach in healthy ways from my addict daughter/son. As I continue to pray about my interactions, I trust You to lead me and give me wisdom.

What can I learn about detaching in a healthy way? How can I love my child in the process?

Waiting

"Behold I stand at the door and knock, if anyone hears my voice and opens the door, I will come in to him and sup with him and he with me." (Revelation 3:20)

It's stunning what people will do to see someone they think important. Some stand in line for hours; others will sleep on the streets overnight to get a ticket to see someone, and that won't be an individual meeting—that will be with thousands of other people. We all would like to have an audience with someone special! We want to feel valued.

It is amazing God waits for us. Incredible that the God of the universe comes knocking on the door of our hearts and invites us to allow Him in. Some might think One as important as God, well, you would have to wait in line, wait your turn—He is the master of the universe; and yet, He asks us if He can come into our hearts and abide with us.

We may feel at times like we are waiting for God. At times, I have felt as if there are things God was not answering or things God was not doing that I had prayed about. In particular, I think of a project of mine, and things were not coming together. I knew that God had asked me to do this; I was acting in obedience to pursue this project, and yet I had hit a wall. God showed me that He was waiting for me!—waiting for me to follow through on other areas of surrender in my life. When I got those things in order, in His time, my project took off in a way I hadn't expected. I had His peace and wisdom about decisions I was making as well. That project was writing!

Don't wait for God; step on in faith and obedience. He's waiting for you!

Prayer

Dear Lord, help me to not keep You waiting but to answer You and to follow Your lead.

Waiting

Is God waiting for you? What do you need to do, and what is stopping you?

Disciplined

"No one serving as a soldier gets entangled in civilian affairs, but rather tries to please his commanding officer. Similarly, anyone who competes as an athlete does not receive the victor's crown except by competing according to the rules." (2 Timothy 2:4-5)

"I can do all things through Christ who gives me strength." (Philippians 4:13)

WHAT COMES TO MIND WHEN YOU THINK OF a soldier? I think of a soldier as regimented, loyal to the cause, respectful of his commanding officer, fully aware of his job description, and recognizable as a soldier. A soldier is always ready for inspection or working at getting things ready for inspection. This picture is of someone who has priorities in place. As with an athlete who is serious about what he or she is doing, this is a disciplined individual with a purpose and single-mindedness toward the goal.

As I think of these qualities, the Holy Spirit brings to mind areas of my life I want to work on. This sounds almost impossible to accomplish. We need Christ's indwelling Spirit helping us to bring our lives into alignment.

Sometimes in our humanness, we don't want to take suggestions or follow the rules, or maybe we don't want to be disciplined. We want to do things our way. This can cause unnecessary challenges in our walks with Christ. We understand that as disciplined people following Christ, as we read God's Word, we learn to follow His lead, not our own.

What a privilege to follow God. What a blessing to have a leader who is worthy of our respect and adoration.

Prayer

Dear Lord, teach me how to follow Your leading and stay true to the course.

Disciplined

What can I change today to become more disciplined in following Christ?

Wisdom

"But the wisdom that comes from heaven is first of all pure, then peace-loving, considerate, submissive, full of mercy and good fruit, impartial and sincere." (James 3:17)

"If any of you lacks wisdom, you should ask God, who gives generously to all without finding fault, and it will be given to you." (James 1:5)

SOME OF THE HARDEST DECISIONS TO MAKE can be ones regarding an adult child with addiction issues. What is helping; what is enabling? How can I be compassionate but not be taken advantage of? I have found that wisdom from God has been my help time and time again.

James talks about wisdom being pure. Only God can make us pure. Pure motives, being pure in heart, and forgiveness for ourselves and others all come from God. Wisdom is peaceful and peace-loving. I think of it as being composed and restful. It is not nervous, irritable, or anxious. Wisdom is considerate, not abrupt or overbearing. It is submissive, teachable, and willing to change. With God's wisdom, I understand other people have weaknesses. With wisdom, I learn to be sincere and transparent.

When I see myself overly worked up and irritable over a decision my addict daughter has made, I am not exercising wisdom that God has for me. Having wisdom has not happened overnight for me, and I doubt it does for most people. I keep practicing. As time goes on, I have seen my growth. I am not as reactionary. I trust God and leave it in His hands first, instead of making it the last thing I do!

We would all like that quick, easy answer to those challenging times when we say, "What do I do now?" Sometimes it's about learning from our mistakes and doing it differently next time. In all situations, God is there to teach us wisdom if we will ask Him.

Prayer

Dear Lord, teach me how to have wisdom. Help me to have the faith to receive wisdom from You.

Wisdom

Is it hard to stop and ask God for wisdom? Is it wise not to?

From Fear to Peace

"Do not be anxious about anything, but in every situation, by prayer and petition with thanksgiving, present your requests to God, and the peace of God which transcends all understanding will guard your hearts and your minds in Christ Jesus." (Philippians 4:6-7)

FEAR HAS GRIPPED MY HEART—FEAR OF where my daughter is and what she is doing when I haven't heard from her for days, fear that she is not going to submit to getting the help she needs, fear of an overdose or a drunken rage or unhealthy behavior when she is high, fear of the consequences that could follow.

Fear and worry go hand in hand. I'm anxious because I don't have control. When I feel I don't have control in my daughter's life, I tend to exercise control in another area of my life. A closet gets cleaned out; a new project is started. Ask my husband—he has witnessed this a time or two! Although it is an effective way to get things done around the house, it doesn't lead me to peace.

There is a way we can get from fear and worry to peace!

First, with faith we look up—we focus on our all-powerful God, not on the challenges around us.

Secondly, we need to saturate ourselves in God's Word. While reading the Word, our faith grows; we are reminded of God's promises, and we can recall God's track record of helping His children. We can trust God; He is more than able.

Thirdly, as we pray, we surrender to the Holy Spirit. As God's Spirit, who is the great Counselor, fills us, we have healing. We read in Romans 15:13, "The God of hope fill you with all joy and peace in believing, that you may abound in hope according to the power of the Holy Spirit within you." It's not something we do for ourselves!

As a result, we have peace; and when we find our hearts filled again by fear and worry, we repeat the above steps. God's peace is there for us.

Prayer

Dear Lord, give us the strength to go through the necessary steps to allow You to work in our lives.

Am I living in fear or in God's peace? What steps do I need to take today?

Healing and Hope

"…a large crowd followed and pressed around him (Jesus), and a woman was there who had been subject to bleeding for 12 years…when she heard about Jesus, she came up behind Him in the crowd and touched His cloak…Jesus realized that power had gone out from Him. He turned around in the crowd and asked, who touched my clothes…the woman knowing what had happened to her, came and fell at His feet, trembling with fear and told Him the truth…He said to her…Go in peace and be free from your suffering." Read the story in its entirety in Mark 5:21-43.

I LOVE THIS STORY BECAUSE I SEE MYSELF IN it. In this story, there is another healing taking place. A synagogue leader named Jairus was pleading with Jesus to come and heal his child. The woman gets healed while Jesus is on His way to heal the child! This speaks to me because as I pray for healing for my child and I believe He is on His way to do it, I receive healing. I am that woman in the crowd, and yet I am also the parent asking and praying for my child who needs healing.

What does the parent of an addict need healing for? For many, it is emotional healing.

A parent of an addict is desperate for God to help and heal his or her child, just like Jairus was desperate for Jesus to heal his child. Jairus probably thought, *Come on, Jesus—why are You waiting to see who touched Your cloak? My child is dying.* We too get impatient with Jesus. He is not working fast enough in our children's lives. He hasn't answered our prayers. Meanwhile, Jesus is healing someone else.

We need to learn how to allow Jesus to heal us as we wait for Him to heal our children. Also, I have learned to accept healing when God gives it. It may be at an unexpected time or different situation than you are prepared for. As we get to know Jesus more and more and as we study Scripture, we learn He quite often does things in a different way than you would expect.

For God to work in the life of an addict, for your child to get better, it's necessary and important that you obey. As we separate from the addicts and get healthy ourselves, this allows the addicts to have their own processes. We will be ready to help the addicts on their journeys. We can obey God and play the role God wants us to play in the addicts' lives only as we are healthy and in the right place with God. I needed to accept that I needed healing.

PRAYER

Dear Lord, teach me to be patient. Show me how to trust Your timing when it comes to being healed. Please help me to accept Your timing and Your healing.

How do I need Jesus to heal me? Have I asked Him for that healing?

Game-Changers

Daily time with God, time in God's Word

Regular fellowship with other believers
   For me, I have a close relationship with sisters in Christ. We meet regularly for Bible study, prayer, and fellowship. The wonderful spiritual healing that occurs from this group can only be from God. *(see below)

Being under the ministry of God's Word, like Bible-based sermons

Learning to be transparent

Reaching out and asking for help or prayer

Accepting help and suggestions

*"Therefore, confess your sins to each other and pray for each other so that you may be healed. The prayer of a person right with God is powerful and effective." (James 5:16)

Recommended Reading

Author James Banks	*Prayers for Prodigals*
Author James Banks	*Praying the Prayers of the Bible*
Author, Geoffrey & James Banks	*Hope Lies Ahead*
Author, Oswald Chambers	*My Utmost for His Highest*
Author, Oswald Chambers	*Prayer, A Holy Occupation*
Author, Oswald Chambers	*Sermon on the Mount*
Author, Gary Chapman	*Five Love Languages*
Author, Mary Ann Froehlich	*Living with Thorns*
Author, Gary Inrig	*Parables of Jesus*
Author, Max Lucado	*Just Like Jesus*
Author, Max Lucado	*Fearless*
Author, Eugene Peterson	*A Long Obedience in the Same Direction*
Author, Roy and Revel	*We Would See Jesus*
Author, David Roper	*Growing Slowly Wise*
Author, David Seamans	*Healing for Damaged Emotions*
Author, A.W. Tozier	*The Pursuit of God*

Author, Warren Wiersbe	*The Bumps Are What You Climb On*
Author, Warren Wiersbe	*Old Testament Words for Today*

About the Author

Kathie Flanders, a graduate in addiction studies and social services, is retired from counseling and from a previous career in banking. Kathie is new to writing and shares that God has been talking to her for some time about journaling and writing about what she has learned as the parent of an adult addict/alcoholic. Kathie is actively involved in a women's Bible group, loves to read, and continues to learn new things from God's Word. A Montana native, Kathie resides in New Hampshire with her husband, where she has lived for over thirty years. She and her husband Dick enjoy traveling in New England, outdoor activities, gardening, and spending time with their grandchildren.

Kathie can be reached at kflanders112@gmail.com.

CPSIA information can be obtained
at www.ICGtesting.com
Printed in the USA
BVHW090805021220
594678BV00014B/1659